MEL BAY PRESENTS
COUNTRY BASS GUITAR MADE EASY
BY LARRY McCABE

Rhythm guitar runs for most of the songs on this recording can be found in Mel Bay's *101 Kickin' Country Rhythm Guitar Runs* by Larry McCabe.

CREDITS

Vocal	Gordon Scott
Bass	Randy Barnhill
Guitar	Larry McCabe
Engineer	Fred Chester
Photos	Becky McCabe, Larry McCabe

CD CONTENTS

1. "A" tuning note

Songs with vocal:
2. Amazing Grace (page 9)
3. All the Good Times (page 10)
4. Angel Band (page 12)
5. Knoxville Girl (page 14)
6. Sweet Hour of Prayer (page 16)
7. Home on the Range (page 18)
8. Wreck of the Old '97 (page 21)
9. Don't Let Your Deal Go Down (page 22)
10. Will the Circle Be Unbroken (page 24)
11. Salty Dog (page 26)
12. Cripple Creek (page 27)
13. Roll in My Sweet Baby's Arms (page 28)
14. Cotton-Eyed Joe (page 30)
15. New River Train (page 32)
16. Wabash Cannonball (page 34)
17. Sinner Man (page 38)
18. The Wayfaring Stranger (page 40)
19. Hangman, Hangman (page 42)
20. Worried Man Blues (page 44)
21. Careless Love (page 46)
22. Corrine, Corrina (page 47)
23. St. James Infirmary (page 48)

"Slowpoke" versions (no vocal):
24. Amazing Grace (page 9)
25. All the Good Times (page 10)
26. Angel Band (page 12)
27. Knoxville Girl (page 14)
28. Sweet Hour of Prayer (page 16)
29. Home on the Range (page 18)
30. Wreck of the Old '97 (page 21)
31. Don't Let Your Deal Go Down (page 22)
32. Will the Circle Be Unbroken (page 24)
33. Salty Dog (page 26)
34. Cripple Creek (page 27)
35. Roll in My Sweet Baby's Arms (page 28)
36. Cotton-Eyed Joe (page 30)
37. New River Train (page 32)
38. Wabash Cannonball (page 34)
39. Sinner Man (page 38)
40. The Wayfaring Stranger (page 40)
41. Hangman, Hangman (page 42)
42. Worried Man Blues (page 44)
43. Careless Love (page 46)
44. Corrine, Corrina (page 47)
45. St. James Infirmary (page 48)

CONTENTS

Introduction 3
How to Use This Book 4
Tuning the Bass 6
How to Read Tablature 7

Songs in 3/4 Time

Amazing Grace (C) 9
All the Good Times Are Past and Gone (G) 10
Angel Band (G) 12
Knoxville Girl (D) 14
Sweet Hour of Prayer (A) 16
Home on the Range (E) 18

Uptempo Songs

Wreck of the Old '97 (C) 21
Don't Let Your Deal Go Down (C) 22
Will the Circle Be Unbroken (G) 24
Salty Dog (G) 26
Cripple Creek (D) 27
Roll in My Sweet Baby's Arms (D) 28
Cotton-Eyed Joe (A) 30
New River Train (A) 32
Wabash Cannonball (E) 34

Minor Keys

Sinner Man (D minor) 38
The Wayfaring Stranger (A minor) 40
Hangman, Hangman (E minor) 42

The Blues

Worried Man Blues (C) 44
Careless Love (G) 46
Corrine, Corrina (E) 47
St. James Infirmary (E minor) 48

APPENDIX: BASIC MUSIC THEORY FOR THE COUNTRY BASS PLAYER 49

INDEX OF TUNES 60

INTRODUCTION

"There once was a butcher named Hutton,
Who had a wife who loved to eat mutton;
   He slipped up behind her
   And pushed her in the grinder,
No Hutton, no mutton, no nuttin'."

"Tell these fine folks another good one, Curly," said the country band leader, Dwayne.

Curly, the group's bass player and comedian, obligingly follows up with a joke about a country parson. Then he tells a funny story about a mixed-up Rhode Island Red hen that lays white eggs only. Pumped up by the enthusiastic chuckling, whistling and knee-slapping in the audience, he wraps up his segment of the program with a little comic jig. The ditty is about an Irish barber living in the Ozarks who drinks shaving lotion when there is no white lightening available for barter.

The setting is Midwestern U.S.A., 1959. Tonight's performance is in a run-down school auditorium in a small town where the Greyhound bus doesn't go. Other shows are put on in big tents in riverbank parks where families have Sunday picnics and Easter egg hunts. Still others take place at fishing tournaments, county fairs, amusement parks, race tracks, rodeo arenas, cattle auctions, rattlesnake roundups, greased-pig chasing contests, Swine Queen festivals, and coyote drives.

Sometimes, after a daytime show or early evening matinee, the boys in the band will be treated to a bonus supper of pan-fried chicken, potato salad, watermelon, ice-cold strawberry soda, and double-stacker devil's food cake. In Wisconsin, fried perch or bratwurst simmered in Old Style beer often replaces the chicken, and cheese biscuits with real butter are served alongside sauerkraut and German potato salad.

Other than being broke all the time, Curly enjoys the traveling band life with Dwayne Dallas and his Buffalo Stompers. He doesn't have to practice much; truth is, the toughest part of his job is hauling the big doghouse bass from town to town. While on the road, the bass is strapped to the roof of Dwayne's old green station wagon with a raggedy old leather mule harness someone found in a barn in Nebraska.

Although his real name is Marvin, having a nickname is an important part of his stage persona, just as it is for other bass-playing country comedians. (Author's note: Had he been chubby, he might have been called "Tiny" or "Slim" instead of "Curly.") On stage, Curly is fitted out with a floppy hat, oversized shoes, a dab of rodeo clown makeup, polka-dot bib overalls, and the obligatory blackened front teeth.

Cheerful and easy-going, he nonetheless visibly resents it when Dwayne allows Lamar, the accordion player, to slip in a joke during a live show. Acknowledging that Lamar is the superior musician, Curly is tenacious in claiming exclusive control over the specialized province of humor, for he has artfully honed his extensive library of backwoods jokes from his boyhood days, when his grandfather would secretly tell him cruel rib-ticklers about the adventures of George Armstrong Custer.

Sadly, Curly is one of the last in the long line of American minstrel entertainers whose roots extend back to the time of Davy Crockett and the Alamo. The Beatles will be here soon, and Curly and his friends will gradually fade into the mists of yesteryear.

1959 was a long time ago, and Curly's time has now passed. Still, it might be fun to think about him now and then while you learn to play country bass guitar. Perhaps you will even be inspired to adopt a nickname and learn a few jokes to tell at a future country gig. After all, being part of the tradition is almost as much fun as the playing itself.

Enjoy the book, and don't let the grass grow under your feet.

Larry McCabe

HOW TO USE THIS BOOK

This book/CD set teaches the basics of country bass guitar in a fun, "quick access" format. In a minimum amount of time, you will learn 22 popular traditional songs including train songs, gospel songs, waltzes, bluegrass songs and country blues. More importantly, the bass patterns that you learn in these songs can be applied to many other country songs, including some of your personal favorites.

The 22 songs in this collection are played in the favorite keys of C, G, D, A, E, A minor, D minor, and E minor. However, if you are a musical beginner, you need not worry if you don't know your key signatures from a wooden nickel. The emphasis here is on quick access, and our agenda is to get you playing entire songs as soon as possible.

The companion CD enables you to "sit in" with a country band that includes a singer, rhythm guitar, and bass. As you play along with the companion recording, you will learn a variety of standard country bass fingering patterns and chord changes. And, if you do want to learn about chords and keys, simply turn to the Appendix (page 49) for an introduction to these and other important musical terms.

The Written Music

The bass part for each song is written in both standard notation and tablature. Tablature allows you to learn tunes even if you do not know how to read music. Located under the music staff, the tablature staff shows the string and fret location of each note. Learning how to read tablature (see page 7) is a simple task that requires only a few minutes.

Having explained the benefits of tablature (foremost of which is immediate gratification), I must also mention that there are even greater benefits in having the ability to read the actual music. These benefits include, but not limited to, the following: 1) The ability to absorb musical information rapidly and accurately; 2) The ability to communicate effectively with musicians in musical settings of all types; 3) The ability to apply abstract principles of music to original compositions and arrangements; 4) The ability to preserve original compositions and arrangements in manuscript form; and 5) The ability to study and understand music at increasingly higher levels.

If you wish to work through a systematic note-reading method for the bass guitar, I recommend Mel Bay's Electric Bass Method by Roger Filberto.

Fingerings

Suggested fretting-hand fingerings are provided in the notation staff. The recommended fingerings are not absolute, and you may modify a particular fingering if you have a better idea.

1 = First (index) finger   2 = Second (middle) finger   3 = Third (ring) finger   4 = Fourth (little) finger

The Companion CD

1. An "A" tuning "beep" is provided on the first track of the companion CD. (Tuning is explained below.) For best results, hold an electronic tuner in front of either speaker to "read" the pitch of the tuning beep.

2. Each song begins with a two-measure chord introduction.

3. Each song is recorded at a moderate speed (tracks 2-23).

4. Each song is also recorded at a "slowpoke" tempo (tracks 24-45) for the benefit of beginners. Each slowpoke track is instrumental only (no singer). The slow instrumental track will help beginners learn to play with the rhythm section without relying on specific lyrics to follow.

5. The bass guitar is isolated in the right speaker. After you gain some experience, turn down the right speaker and try to devise your own bass patterns.

Procedure

The songs are organized in the book by style (uptempo, 3/4 time, etc.) and key, not by level of difficulty. If you are a beginner, I recommend that you start with the following **super-easy** songs in the following order:

1) "Cripple Creek" (page 29)
2) "All the Good Times Are Past and Gone" (page 12)
3) "Cotton-Eyed Joe" (page 32)
4) "Sweet Hour of Prayer" (page 18)
5) "Amazing Grace" (page 10)
6) "Wreck of the Old '97" (page 23)
7) "Knoxville Girl" (page 16)
8) "Sinner Man" (page 40)

After that, you can work through the songs in any order. Players with prior experience can learn the tunes in any order according to personal preference.

It will help you a lot if you listen to the recording of the song you are about to learn. Sing along with the bass part, and try to memorize it before you learn from the music. Also, read the brief performance tips and comments that accompany each song. In music, concept precedes technique, and technique precedes expression. Always know what you are supposed to do before you try to do it. After that, practice until the performance is polished to your personal satisfaction.

Regardless of your level of ability, you may at some point encounter a tune that is too difficult (although that is unlikely in this book). If this happens, try another song and return to the more challenging example later.

Scales and Keys and Chords

After you have learned a tune or two, you might want to learn some musical concepts that will help you understand what you are playing. If so, please see the Appendix beginning on page 49. This section discusses important music basics such as scales, keys, and chords, in everyday language that is easy to understand.

Having a conceptual understanding of the materials of music will enable you to avoid the fragmented "rote" approach that is often the result of neglecting the basics. For example, if you know the scale you are (supposed to be) playing in a given song, you will have a visual "roadmap" of the most important tones of the moment. In addition, knowing the scale position of the tones that are used to go from one chord to another will help you apply these sounds to chord changes in various keys. Knowing the notes in the scales and chords also helps you learn what not to play.

To Pick or Not to Pick

Some bass players pluck the strings with the index and middle fingers; others use a plastic guitar pick. If you are an absolute beginner, and you do not have access to a qualified teacher, consider using a pick for at least your first few tunes. If you wish to play with the fingers of the picking hand rather than a pick (I'm not advocating one approach over the other), study a graded bass guitar method such as Mel Bay's Electric Bass Method. This will teach you the proper technique of using the fingers of the picking hand.

The following symbols, used occasionally in this book, indicate the motion of the pick.

⊓ Pick down   V Pick up

TUNING THE BASS

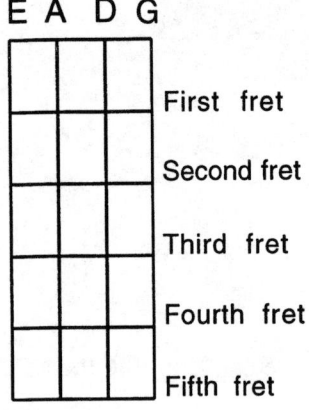

The diagram at the left shows the four strings (represented by the vertical lines) and the first five frets (represented by the horizontal lines) on a standard four-string bass guitar. The strings are named E (this is the biggest string), A, D, and G (this is the smallest string).

• The easiest and most accurate way to tune is with an *electronic tuner* which can be purchased at any music store or from Mel Bay Publications. The tuner "reads" the pitch of each string and tells you when the string is properly tuned.

• You can also tune to a *pitch pipe*. This is a small reed instrument that sounds the pitch to each string. However, you must match the pitch of the string to the pitch pipe, and doing this is very difficult for most beginners. Still, a pitch pipe is handy for reference.

• *Relative tuning,* also called *desert island tuning*, is achieved as follows:

1. Tune the fifth fret of the D string to match the open G string. Fret (hold down) the fifth fret of the D string (with any finger), checking the pitch of the fifth fret against the open G string. If the fifth fret sounds higher than the open G string, detune the D string by winding the tuning key a fraction of a turn. Then check the notes again, continuing in this manner until the notes match.

   If the fretted note sounds lower than the open G string, tune the string up (by winding the tuning key in the appropriate direction). Check the notes, and continue the process until a satisfactory match has been achieved.

2. Tune the fifth fret of the A string to match the open D string. Follow the procedure described above.

3. Tune the fifth fret of the E string to match the open A string. Again, follow the procedure described above.

• Some students may wish to tune the bass to a piano or keyboard instrument. The pitch of each open string is shown in the music staff below.*

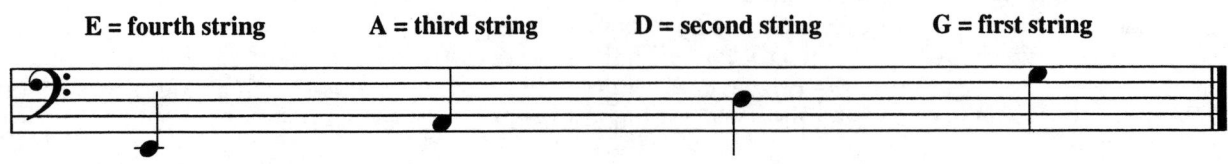

Each string can be called by either its name or its number. For example, E, the lowest-sounding string, is the fourth string. G, the highest-pitched string, is the first string.

* Technically, music for the bass is written an octave higher than it actually sounds. But these tones will still do for tuning.

HOW TO READ TABLATURE

1. The *music staff* is marked by the bass clef symbol: 𝄢
2. The *tablature staff* is marked by the word "TAB."
3. Unlike standard music notation, each line of the tablature staff represents a string.
4. The <u>top line</u> of the tablature staff represents the <u>first string</u>. This is the highest-pitched string.
5. The <u>second line</u> from the top represents the <u>second string</u>.
6. The <u>third line</u> from the top represents the <u>third string</u>.
7. The <u>lowest line</u> represents the lowest or <u>fourth string</u>.

8. A "0" (zero) on any tablature line tells you to play that string "open." "Open" means to play the string without placing any fingers on it.

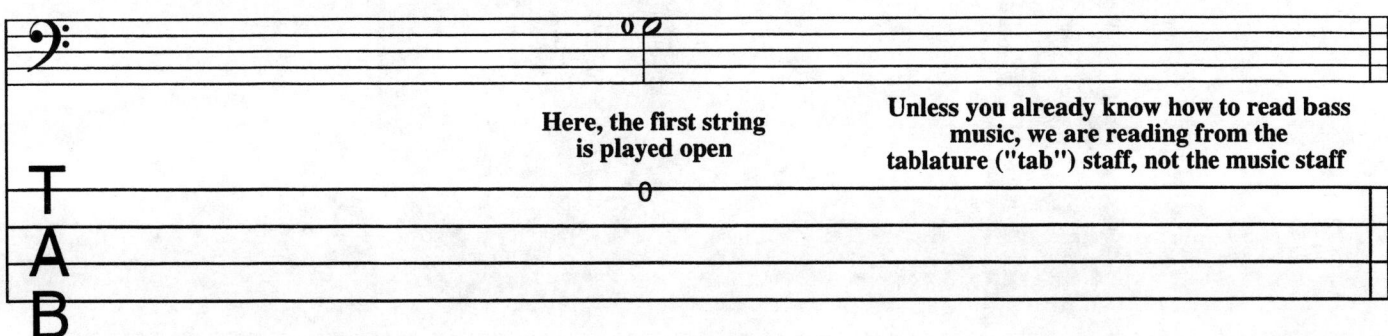

Here, the first string is played open

Unless you already know how to read bass music, we are reading from the tablature ("tab") staff, not the music staff

9. A <u>number</u> on a "tab" line tells you what fret to play. For example, a 2 on the top line tells you to play the second fret of the first string. The 2 represents the fret, and the top line represents the first string.

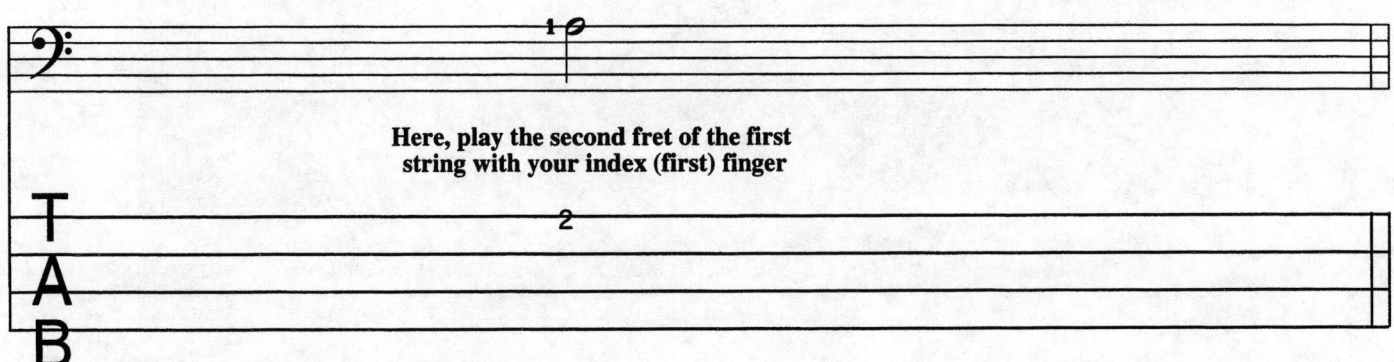

Here, play the second fret of the first string with your index (first) finger

Songs in 3/4 Time

All the Good Times Are Past and Gone

This song uses only the *primary chords* in the key of G major: G, C, D, and D7. The bass part is very easy and you should be able to master it in a short amount of time.

"All the Good Times are Past and Gone" begins with a 16-measure verse, followed by a 16-measure chorus. The *verse-chorus* song form is used in thousands of folk and country songs both new and traditional.

TRACK 3 (VOCAL)
TRACK 25 (SLOW)

© 2006 by Mel Bay Publications (BMI). All Rights Reserved.

Oh, can you hear that lonesome train,
A-comin' round the bend;
It's going to take me 'way from here,
N'er to return again. (Chorus)

Oh, don't you see that lonesome dove,
Who flies from pine to pine;
He's mourning for his own true love,
Just like I mourn for mine. (Chorus)

Angel Band

"Angel Band," like the previous song "All the Good Times Are Past and Gone," contains only the three primary chords in the key of G. In this arrangement, however, there is more motion in the bass from chord to chord. To learn a little about bass variations on the same chord changes, compare the first four measures of "All the Good Times Are Past and Gone" to the first four bars of "Angel Band."

Notice also that "Angel Band" has a "true" chorus in which both the melody and chord progression are different than the melody and chord progression of the verse.

TRACK 4 (VOCAL)
TRACK 26 (SLOW)

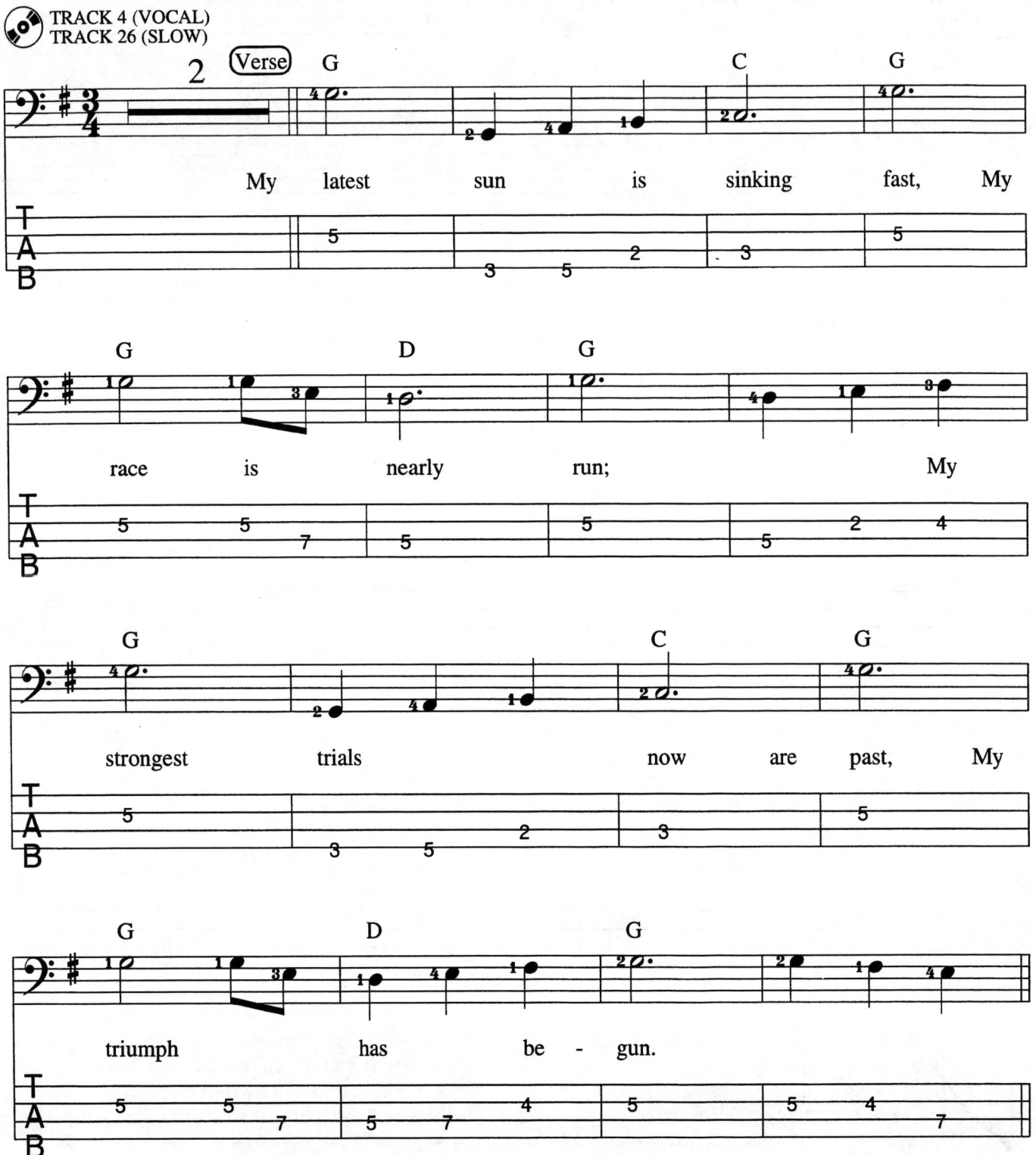

© 2006 by Mel Bay Publications (BMI). All Rights Reserved.

Knoxville Girl

"Knoxville Girl," a tragic American ballad, is arranged here in the key of D. The three primary chords in this key are D, G, and A (or A7). Other chords used in this song are D7 and E7. The D7 chord (I7) (measures 4 and 18) connects the I chord (D) to the IV chord (G); E7 (II7) (measures 13-14) connects the I chord (D) to the V7 chord (A7). I7 and II7 are known as *secondary dominant* chords.

The chord changes I-I7-IV and I-II7-V or V7 are standard changes in all major keys.

"Knoxville Girl" is a 32-bar *AAA* (verses only) song.

After you learn this arrangement, experiment with other fingerings for the bass line. The suggested fingerings are not absolute, so feel free to substitute other fingerings that you feel are logical.

TRACK 5 (VOCAL)
TRACK 27 (SLOW)

© 2006 by Mel Bay Publications (BMI). All Rights Reserved.

Sweet Hour of Prayer

"Sweet Hour of Prayer" is played here in the key of A major. A, D, and E are the three primary chords in this key. The A/C# chord symbol in measures 17 and 21 is a *slash chord* symbol for an A major chord with a C# note in the bass.

The form for this song is AABA. An AABA song has two distinct parts, A and B. The A section is played first, then it is repeated. Next, the B section is played, followed by another A section which closes the completed "chorus." Each section is eight measures long; this is the standard section length for AABA tunes. The four eight-bar sections produce a full "chorus" of 32-bars.

The B section in AABA songs is sometimes mistakenly called a chorus.

American Hymn
Mid-1800s
Wm. W. Walford
Wm. B. Bradbury

TRACK 6 (VOCAL)
TRACK 28 (SLOW)

© 2006 by Mel Bay Publications (BMI). All Rights Reserved.

16

Sweet Hour of Prayer, Sweet Hour of Prayer,
Thy wings shall my petition bear;
To Him whose truth and faithfulness,
Engage the waiting soul to bless.
And since He bids me seek His face,
Believe His Word, and trust His grace;
I'll cast on Him my every care,
And wait for thee, Sweet Hour of Prayer.

Where the air is so pure and the zephyrs so free,
And the breezes so balmy and light;
I would not exhange my Home on the Range,
Not for all of the cities so bright. (Chorus)

How often at night when the heavens are bright,
With the light of the glittering stars;
I stood there amazed and I asked as I gazed,
If their glory exceeds that of ours. (Chorus)

Uptempo Songs

Don't Let Your Deal Go Down

This song introduces the *cycle of fourths* chord progression A7 - D7 - G7 - C. Translated to The Nashville number system (for use in any major key), the progression is VI7 - II7 - V7 - I.

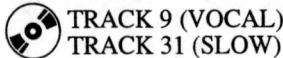
TRACK 9 (VOCAL)
TRACK 31 (SLOW)

Been all a-round this whole wide world,

Way down to Memphis, Tennes-see;

Any old place that I hang my hat

Seems like home to me.

© 2006 by Mel Bay Publications (BMI). All Rights Reserved.

Will the Circle Be Unbroken

The chord progression is the same in both the verse and chorus. Compare the bass parts in the two sections.

TRACK 10 (VOCAL)
TRACK 32 (SLOW)

Salty Dog

"Salty Dog" uses the cycle of fourths chord progression introduced in "Don't Let Your Deal Go Down," VI7 - II7 - V7 - I. In this key (G), the numbers translate to E7 - A7 - D7 - G.

TRACK 11 (VOCAL)
TRACK 33 (SLOW)

Look here, Sal, I know you,
Run down stockin's and wore-out shoes;
Honey, let me be your Salty Dog!
(Chorus)

Down in the wildwood sittin' on a log,
Finger on the trigger and an eye on the hog;
Honey, let me be your Salty Dog!
(Chorus)

Pulled the trigger and the gun said, "go,"
The shot fell over in Mexico;
Honey, let me be your Salty Dog!
(Chorus)

© 2006 by Mel Bay Publications (BMI). All Rights Reserved.

Cripple Creek

The standard version of "Cripple Creek" uses three chords. This old-time version, closely related to the tune "Ida Red," uses only two chords, I (D) and V7 (A7).
The entire arrangement can be played using only the first finger of the fretting hand.

TRACK 12 (VOCAL)
TRACK 34 (SLOW)

Well, the easiest money that ever I made, I made up in Cripple Creek layin' in the shade; Girls up in Cripple Creek a-bout half grown, Jump on a man like a dog on a bone. Goin' up Cripple Creek, Goin' in a run, Goin' up Cripple Creek to have a little fun.

I got a gal at the head of the creek,	Cripple Creek's wide, Cripple Creek's deep,	You get a line, I'll get a pole,
Goin' up to see her in the middle of the week;	I'll wade old Cripple Creek 'fore I sleep;	Go right down to the fishin' hole;
Goin' up Cripple Creek, goin' in a wiz,	Roll my britches to my knees,	Big old turtle seen a duck,
Goin' up Cripple Creek to see little Liz.	I'll wade old Cripple Creek when I please.	Pulled him under and had a snack.
(Chorus)	(Chorus)	(Chorus)

© 2006 by Mel Bay Publications (BMI). All Rights Reserved.

Roll in My Sweet Baby's Arms

"Roll in My Sweet Baby's Arms," a song with great audience appeal, has been recorded by many groups. This bass part is influenced by Buck Owen's version on the album Ruby and Other Bluegrass Specials. The verse and chorus, each 16 bars in length, are based on the same chord progression.

TRACK 13 (VOCAL)
TRACK 35 (SLOW)

Cotton-Eyed Joe

A perennial favorite with dancers and fiddlers alike, "Cotton-Eyed Joe" is usually played in the key of A. Like many fiddle songs, the tune is called an *AB tune* when it is played instrumentally. The first section of the tune is the A section, and the second section is the B section.

Cornstalk fiddle and a cornstalk bow,
Cotton-Eyed Joe there jiggin' on the floor.
(Chorus)

Gonna load up my old forty-four,
Get a little supper for the folks comin' oer.
(Chorus)

Jumped out of bed and stumped my toe,
Call the doctor, Cotton-Eyed Joe.
(Chorus)

© 2006 by Mel Bay Publications (BMI). All Rights Reserved.

New River Train

A key distinguishing feature between a chorus in a verse-chorus song and a B section in an AABA song (see "Sweet Hour of Prayer," page 18) is this: a song can start with a chorus, but not with a B section. "New River Train," a verse-chorus song, begins with the chorus.

This bass line uses more notes than the previous songs. The pattern played to the A chord in measures 1-2, 3-4, and 20-21 is an important pattern that works with both major and dominant chords. We call this pattern a 1-3-5-3 pattern because it uses the 1-3-5-3 notes of the scale.

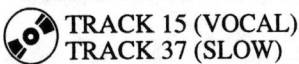
TRACK 15 (VOCAL)
TRACK 37 (SLOW)

© 2006 by Mel Bay Publications (BMI). All Rights Reserved.

Darlin', you can't love two,
Darlin', you can't love two;
You can't love two and your little heart be true,
Darlin' you can't love two. (Chorus)

Darlin', you can't love three,
Darlin', you can't love three;
You can't love three and still love me,
Darlin', you can't love three. (Chorus)   Etc.

Wabash Cannonball

Most verse-chorus songs have 16 bars in each section. However, there are times when an "extra" measure is added to this standard length. Such is the case with "Wabash Cannonball," which has 17 measures in both the verse and the chorus. The extra measure is found more often in bluegrass songs than in commercial country music.

The D# note in measure 17 of the verse is known as a *lower neighbor* tone. A lower neighbor is an *approach tone* that is 1/2 step below the root of the chord it is moving to. Lower neighbors are used quite often in bass playing, and you will find others in this book if you take a few minutes to analyze some of the songs.

TRACK 16 (VOCAL)
TRACK 38 (SLOW)

© 2006 by Mel Bay Publications (BMI). All Rights Reserved.

Oh, the Eastern states are dandy, so the people always say,
From New York to Saint Louis and Chicago by the way;
From the hills of Minnesota where the rippling waters fall,
No changes can be taken on the Wabash Cannonball.
(Chorus)

She came down from Birmingham one cold December day,
When she pulled into the station you could hear all the people say;
There's a girl from Tennessee here, she's long and she's tall,
She came down from Birmingham on the Wabash Cannonball.
(Chorus)

Minor Keys

Sinner Man

The traditional hymn "Sinner Man" evokes the spirit of Jonathan Edwards' "Sinners in the Hands of an Angry God," a famous fire-and-brimstone sermon from the time of the Great Awakening (ca. 1734-1760). Adding to the eeriness of the lyrics is the minor key setting, but the weirdness is offset somewhat by an upbeat performance tempo (the song is played at a moderate tempo on the companion CD).

The primary chords in D minor are Dm (im), Gm (ivm), and Am (vm). V7 is frequently substituted for vm in the minor keys (both vm and V7 can be used in the same song). F (♭III), B♭ (♭VI), and C (♭VII) are the secondary chords in this key. "Sinner Man" uses only the im-♭VII chords, D minor and C.

D natural minor is the *relative minor* of the key of F major.

TRACK 17 (VOCAL)
TRACK 39 (SLOW)

Oh, Sinner Man, where you gonna run to? Oh, Sinner Man, where you gonna run to? Oh, Sinner Man, where you gonna run to, All on that day?

© 2006 by Mel Bay Publications (BMI). All Rights Reserved.

Verse

Dm
Run to the Lord, Lord, won't you hide me?

C
Run to the Lord, Lord, won't you hide me?

Dm
Run to the Lord, Lord, won't you hide me,

Dm **C** **Dm** **Dm**
All on that day?

Don't make a sound, the devil's gonna hear you, (3x)
All on that day. (Chorus)

Dig in the ground, the devil's gonna catch you, (3x)
All on that day. (Chorus)

Run to the rock, the rock was a meltin', (3x)
All on that day. (Chorus)

Run to the sea, the sea was a boiling, (3x)
All on that day. (Chorus)

The Wayfaring Stranger

"The Wayfaring Stranger," based on an Irish tune, is one of the best-known Appalachian hymns. The mournful lyrics tell of a person who anticipates trading the sorrows of this life for the heavenly rewards of the next one. Burl Ives, the great folksinger and actor, used the song title for his 1948 autobiography.

This arrangement is played in the key of A natural minor. The principal chords in this key are Am (im), C (bIII), Dm (ivm), Em (vm), F (bVI), and G (bVII). E7 (V7) is frequently substituted for Em. Four of the principal chords (Am, Dm, F, and C) are played here. Perform the song with a moderate, bluesy shuffle beat.

The song form is AABC.

TRACK 18 (VOCAL)
TRACK 40 (SLOW)

I am a poor Wayfaring Stranger, Traveling through this world of woe; But there's no sorrow no toil or danger, In that bright world to which I go. I'm going

© 2006 by Mel Bay Publications (BMI). All Rights Reserved.

Lyrics under the music:

there — to see my father, I'm going
there — no more to roam; I'm only
go - ing over Jordan, I'm just
go - ing over home.

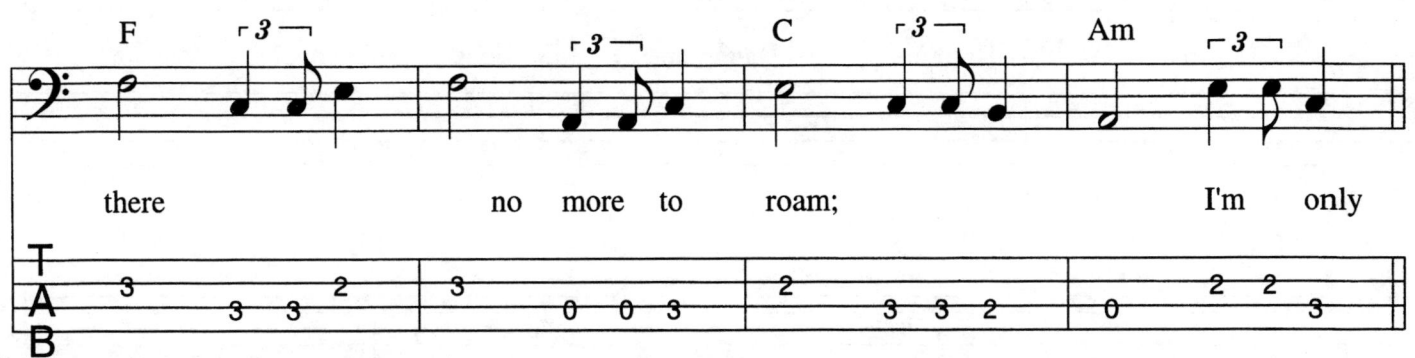

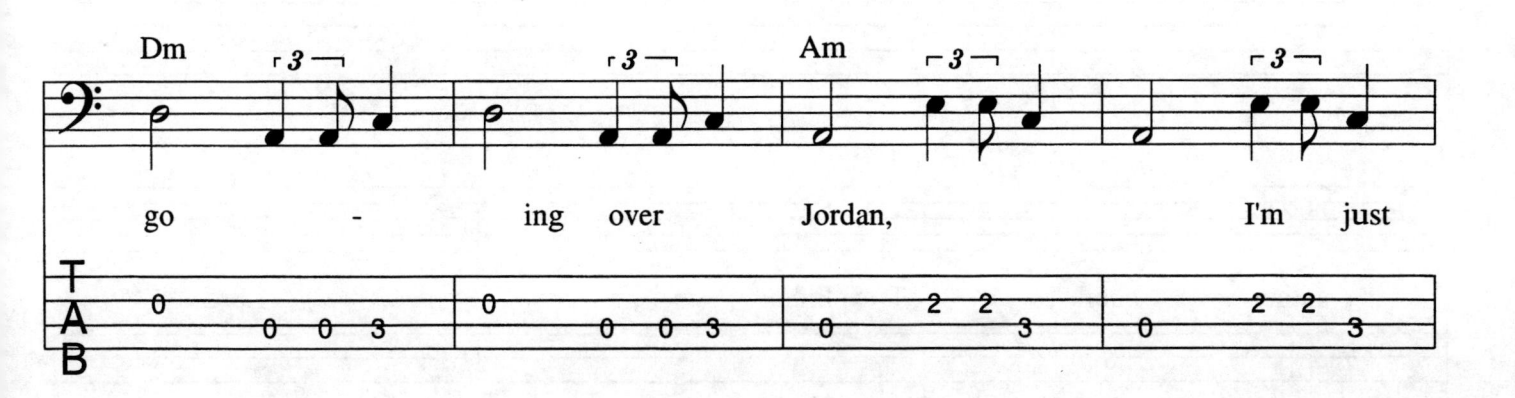

I know dark clouds will gather 'round me,
My way is rough and steep, I know;
But golden fields lie just before me,
In that fair land to which I go.

I'm going there see my mother,
I'm goin' there no more to roam;
I'm goin' there just over Jordan,
I'm goin' there to my new home.

Hangman, Hangman

Known variously as "Hangman, Hangman," "Hangman," "Gallows Pole," and "The Maid Freed From the Gallows," this famous British ballad is performed here in E minor. Like most traditional songs, there are many versions of this tune. "Hangman" is sometimes performed in a major key. Peter, Paul and Mary sang a wonderful major-key arrangement of the song on their 1965 See What Tomorrow Brings album.

Our arrangement uses all six principal chords in the key of E minor, with B7 (V7) substituting for Bm (vm).

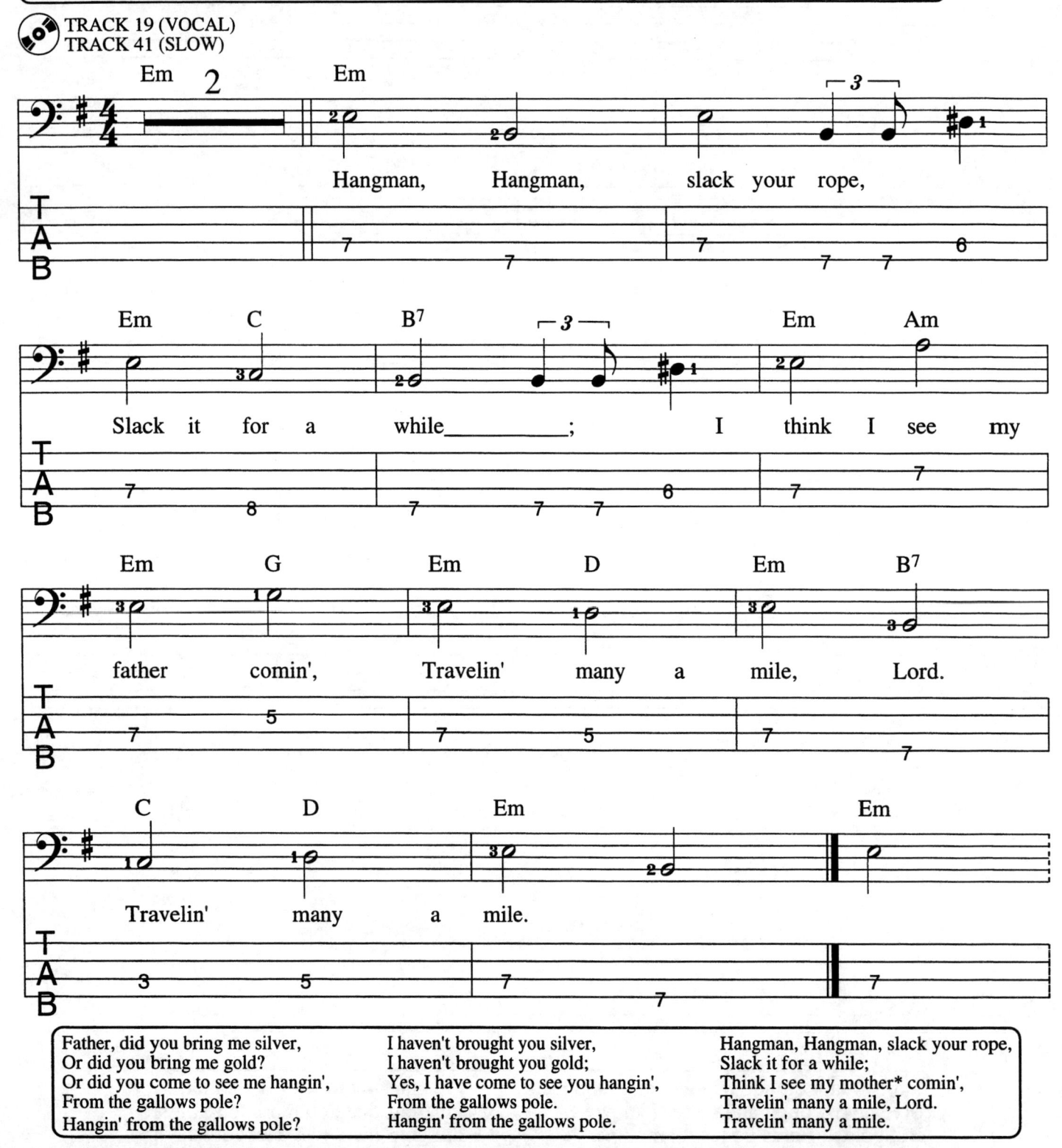

TRACK 19 (VOCAL)
TRACK 41 (SLOW)

Hangman, Hangman, slack your rope,
Slack it for a while_____; I think I see my
father comin', Travelin' many a mile, Lord.
Travelin' many a mile.

Father, did you bring me silver,
Or did you bring me gold?
Or did you come to see me hangin',
From the gallows pole?
Hangin' from the gallows pole?

I haven't brought you silver,
I haven't brought you gold;
Yes, I have come to see you hangin',
From the gallows pole.
Hangin' from the gallows pole.

Hangman, Hangman, slack your rope,
Slack it for a while;
Think I see my mother* comin',
Travelin' many a mile, Lord.
Travelin' many a mile.

Note: In most versions of the song, the protagonist is rescued in the last verse.

* Brother, sister, lover, etc.

© 2006 by Mel Bay Publications (BMI). All Rights Reserved.

Blues

Worried Man Blues

"Worried Man Blues" is based on the basic *12-bar blues progression*. Thousands of country, blues, folk, jazz, bluegrass, and popular songs are based on blues progressions.

Expressed in Roman numerals, the basic blues progression looks like this:
(See page 56 for an explanation of the Roman numeral system.)

I	I	I	I
IV	IV	I	I
V7	V7	I	I

Most blues songs consist of only a 12-bar verse. In this song, both the verse and chorus use the same blues progression.

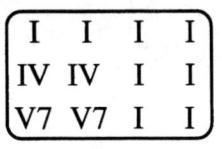

TRACK 20 (VOCAL)
TRACK 42 (SLOW)

I went across the river I lay down to sleep, I went across the river and I lay down to sleep; When I woke up had shackles on my feet. It

© 2006 by Mel Bay Publications (BMI). All Rights Reserved.

Chorus

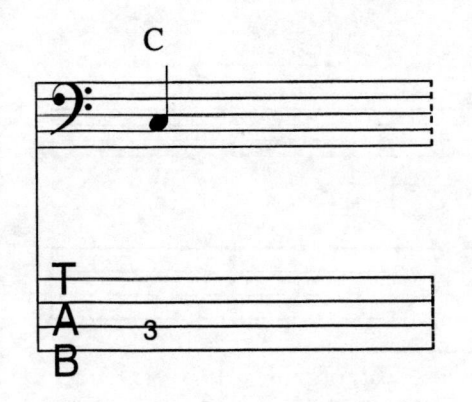

takes a worried man to sing a worried song, It
takes a worried man to sing a worried song; I'm worried
now but I won't be worried long.

Careless Love

"Careless Love" is a perennial blues favorite that has been played in all major styles. The earliest published lyrics to the song appeared in Journal of American Folklore in 1911. In that publication the song was called "Kelly's Love."

Although the song's 16-bar verse is not a standard 12-bar blues progression, the lyrics, lightly syncopated melody, and the overall mood of the song qualify it as a blues nonetheless.

This arrangement features typical blues finger patterns and a shuffle rhythm. Listen carefully to the companion CD to get the feel for this rhythm. Divide each beat into a triplet (three even parts), playing the first of a pair of eighth notes on the first triplet, and the second eighth note on the third triplet.

TRACK 21 (VOCAL)
TRACK 43 (SLOW)

Love, oh love, oh Careless Love.

Love, oh love, oh Careless Love;

Love, oh love, oh Careless Love, Can't you

see what love has done to me.

I cried last night and the night before,
Cried last night and the night before;
I cried last night and the night before,
Gonna cry tonight and cry no more.

It's gone and broke this heart of mine,
Gone and broke this heart of mine;
It's gone and broke this heart of mine,
It'll break that heart of yours sometime.

© 2006 by Mel Bay Publications (BMI). All Rights Reserved.

Corrine, Corrina

Combining the standard blues progression of "Worried Man Blues" with the 4-beat *walking bass* style used in "Careless Love," "Corrine, Corrina" is arranged here as a 12-bar *shuffle* blues. The shuffle beat is the most popular blues rhythm.

A shuffle beat is divided into three parts (trip-a-let) instead of two (one-and). The first note of a pair of eighth notes receives 2/3 of the beat (trip-a); the second note of the pair receives 1/3 of the beat (-let).

TRACK 22 (VOCAL)
TRACK 44 (SLOW)

Corrine, Cor - rina, Where you been so long? Corrine, Cor-rina, Where you been so long? Ain't had no lovin', Since you been gone.

Corrine, Corrina, where'd you stay last night?
Corrine, Corrina, where'd you stay last night?
Come in this mornin',
Sun was shinin' bright.

I love Corrina, tell the world I do.
I love Corrina, tell the world I do.
Just a little more lovin',
Make your heart beat true.

Goodbye Corrina, it's fare-the-well.
Goodbye Corrina, it's fare-the-well.
When I come back babe,
Lord, you never can tell.

© 2006 by Mel Bay Publications (BMI). All Rights Reserved.

St. James Infirmary

There are several titles to this famous 8-bar blues, including "Gambler's Blues" and "Old Joe's Barroom." In addition, there exist many various lyrics for this song, and they are about as morbid as they come.

"St. James Infirmary" is arranged here in the key of E minor. The simple harmony is based on the three primary chords, Em (im), Am (ivm), and B7 (V7).

TRACK 23 (VOCAL)
TRACK 45 (SLOW)

I went down to St. James In - firmary,
Saw my baby there; Stretched out on a cold white
table, So sweet, so cold, so fair.

Went up to see the doctor,	Well, I tried to keep from cryin',	When I die, please dress me in the new look,
"Can't help you, son," he said;	My heart felt just like lead;	With a fancy coat and a real-gone hat;
When I went back to see my woman,	She was all I had to live for,	Put a twenty-carat gold ring on my finger,
She had left for another world.	I wish that it was me instead.	And have a jazz band play the "Skit-Dee-Doo-Skat."

© 2006 by Mel Bay Publications (BMI). All Rights Reserved.

Appendix

Basic Theory for the Country Bass Player

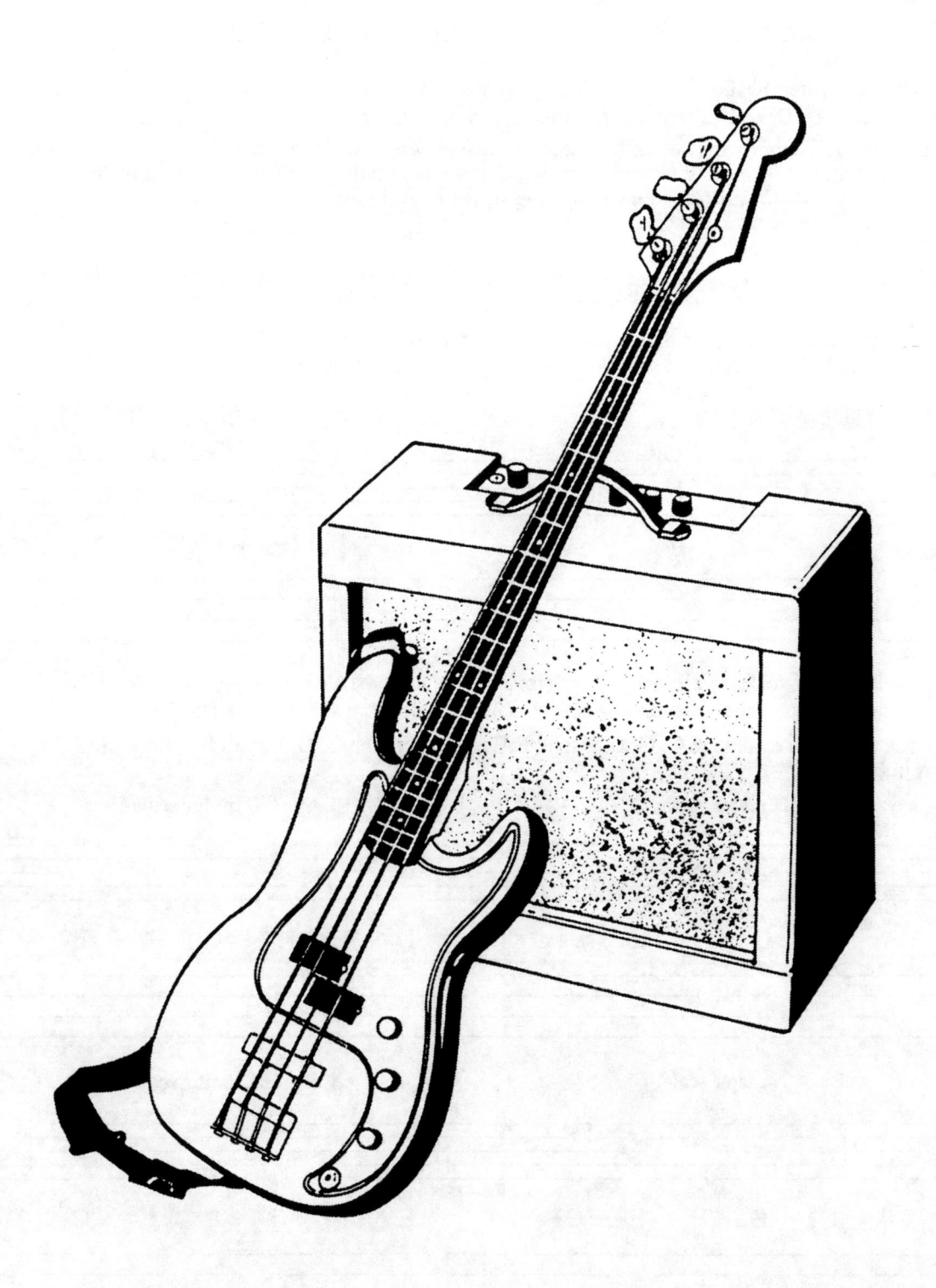

Appendix
Basic Music Theory for the Country Bass Player

The Western System

Most American popular music is based on the *Western music system.* This means that the origins of today's American music can be found in European (and later, American) music. The Western system (we are not specifically referring to the American country-western style when we use this term) is based on twelve musical tones (the terms *tone* and *note* are used interchangeably in this discussion):

A, B flat (or A sharp), B, C, D flat (or C sharp), D, E flat (or D sharp), E, F, G flat (or F sharp), G, A flat (or G sharp).

The *flat* notes are written B♭, D♭, and so on. The *sharp* notes are written C♯, F♯, etc. Some notes have two names (B♭ and A♯; D♭ and C♯; etc.); these notes are called *enharmonic* notes.

The origins of today's country music can be traced to the folk songs of England, Ireland, and Scotland. For example, the tune to "Amazing Grace" is known in Ireland, and the words were written by an Englishman who moved to America in the early days of the new country.

The Major Scale

It is said that music is language of sound. Just as a spoken language is based on letters and words, music is based on *scales*. A musical *scale* is an organized series of several (usually five to seven) musical tones.

There are many types of scales, but the *major scale* is the most important one. The C major scale is shown in Ex. 1. The C scale contains only *natural* notes; there are no sharps or flats in this scale.

Ex. 1 The tones in the C major scale

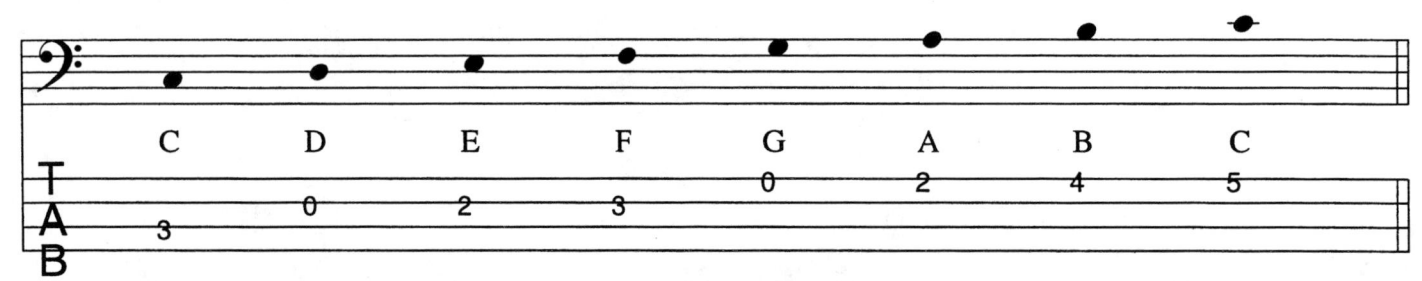

There are twelve major scales in all, one for each tone. Every major scale has seven tones. With the exception of the C major scale, each major scale contains one or more sharped or flatted tones.

The most popular major scales are C, G, D, A, and E. The tones in the G, D, A, and E major scales are shown in Ex. 2 - 5.

Ex. 2 G major scale

Ex. 3 D major scale

Ex. 4 A major scale

Ex. 5 E major scale

The Natural Minor Scale

The *natural minor scale* is another scale that you should know. This scale is important in almost all types of music. The notes in the *A natural minor scale* are shown in Ex. 6. Examine the notes in this scale, and you will see that they are the same notes that make up the C major scale.

Ex. 6 The tones in the A natural minor scale

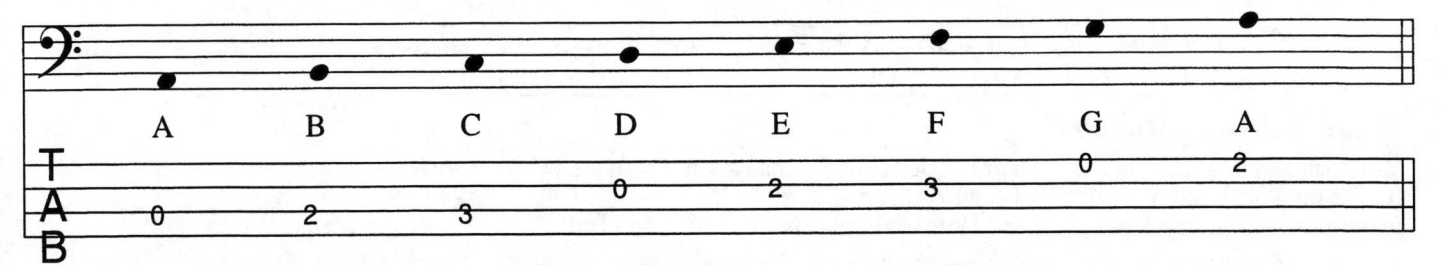

Because the A natural minor scale uses the tones in the C major scale, it is known as the *relative minor* of C major. Likewise, the C major scale is known as the *relative major* of A natural minor. One way to think of the natural minor scale: it is "generated" from the sixth tone of its relative major scale. For example, the first tone in the A natural minor scale (A) is also the sixth tone of the C major scale (C-D-E-F-G-A-B-C).

Examples 7-12 show the relative minor scales of the following major scales: G, D, A, and E.

Ex. 7 E natural minor is related to G major

Ex. 8 B minor is related to D major

Ex. 9 F♯ minor is related to A major

Ex. 10 C♯ minor is related to E major

The most common natural minor scales in simple music are A minor, E minor, and D minor. The D natural minor scale (Ex. 11) is related to the F major scale (Ex. 12).

Ex. 11 The D natural minor scale

Ex. 12 The F major scale

> There are twelve natural minor scales in all, one for each tone.
>
> The natural minor scale is also called the *Aeolian* scale (or mode). The major scale is also called the *Ionian* scale (or mode). *Mode* is another word for scale.

Intervals

The distance from one note to another is called an *interval*. Let's learn to identify simple intervals on the bass.

The distance of one fret is called a *half-step*. Thus, the second fret is a half-step higher than the first fret, but half a step lower than the third fret. <u>Two</u> half-steps make a *whole step*. An interval of a whole step represents the distance of two frets on the bass guitar. For example, the note on the third fret (on any string) is a whole step higher than the note on the first fret (on the same string).

> Examples of half-step intervals: E to F; B to C. Can you find others?
> Examples of whole-step intervals: C to D; F to G. Can you find others?

Major Scale Construction

You may have noticed that each major scale (above) sounds similar to the others, even though each scale begins on a different note. This is because each major scale is constructed according to the same pattern of intervals: Whole - Whole - Half - Whole - Whole - Whole - Half.

Knowing that each type of scale is constructed according to the same pattern of intervals tells us why some scales require *accidental* notes (sharps and flats).

Example 13 shows an easy way to visualize the pattern of intervals in the C major scale: Simply play the notes of the scale in succession on a single string (see the tablature for Ex. 13).

Ex. 13 C major scale on the third string

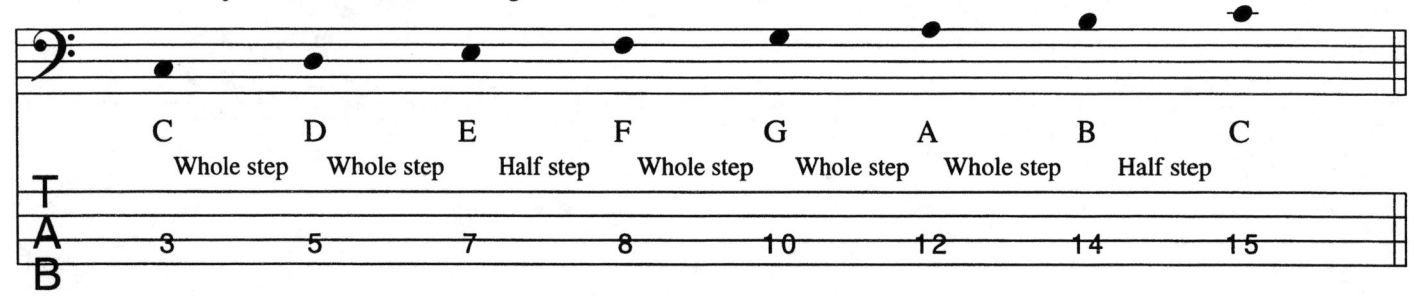

Tonic Note

The first note in any scale is called the *tonic* note. The second tone in a major scale is always one step above the tonic.

Major Keys

Every song we play is set in a particular "tone center" known as a *key*. For example, "Amazing Grace" is played in the *key of C major*, and "Careless Love" is played in the *key of G major* in this book. A song played in a given major key is based on the notes of the corresponding major scale. For example, the melody to "Amazing Grace," played in the key of C major, contains only notes found in the C major scale.

Each key is identified by a *key signature* which appears just after the clef sign. The key signature shows the sharps or flats of the corresponding major scale (Ex. 14). Of course, there are no sharps or flats for the key of C, because there are no sharps or flats in the C major scale.

Ex. 14 Key signatures for the five popular major keys

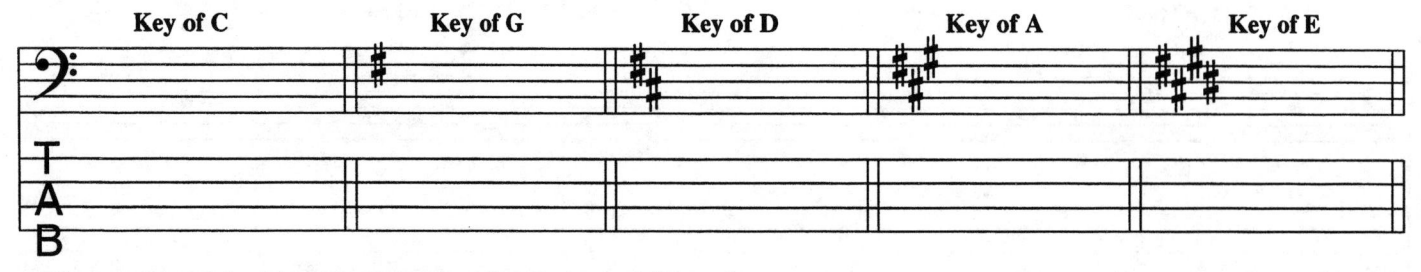

The concept of the key is broader than the concept of the scale:

1. The notes in the scale are "fixed." For instance, the notes in the C scale are C, D, E, F, G, A, B, C. Notes having other names do not belong to this scale.

2. The key tells us what the "main notes" are (the notes in the corresponding scale). However, the key also permits us to use other notes. In a simple song in the key of C, we might use only notes from the C scale. A more complex song in the key of C would use the C scale as its foundation, but other notes would also be used.

Natural Minor Scale Construction

The natural minor scale is constructed according to the following pattern of intervals:

Whole - Half - Whole - Whole - Half - Whole - Whole.

If you played some of the scales on the previous pages, you probably noticed that the major scales have a different sound than the natural minor scales. This is because each scale type contains its own unique pattern of intervals.

The natural minor scale contains both a *flatted third* and a *flatted seventh* tone. The flatted third can also be called a *minor third* interval, and the flatted seventh can be called a *minor seventh* interval. Both of these intervals are discussed on the next page.

Example 15 shows an easy way to visualize the pattern of intervals in the A natural minor scale by playing the notes of the scale along the length of the third string (Ex. 15, tablature).

Ex. 15 <u>A natural minor</u> scale on the third string

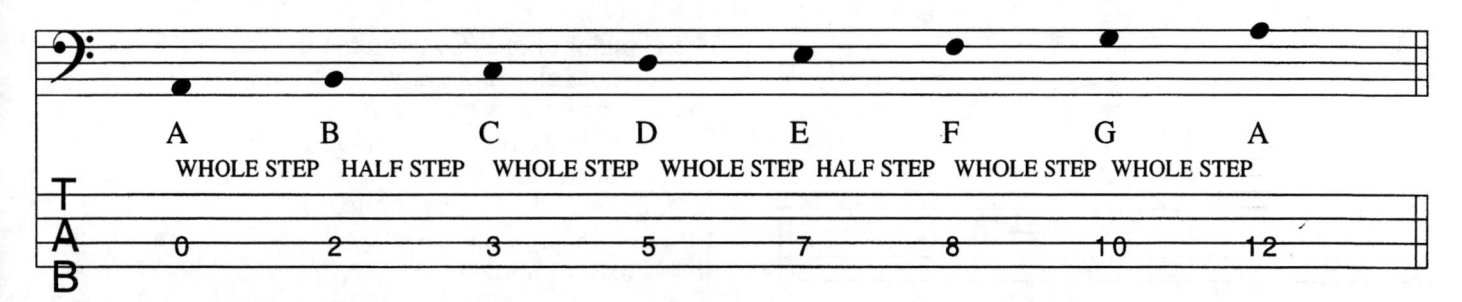

Minor Keys

Every major key has a *relative minor key*. Each relative minor key is based on the tones of the corresponding relative minor scale. For example, songs in the key of A natural minor are based on the tones of the A natural minor scale.

The three most popular minor keys (Ex. 16) are:

The key of A minor. This key is the relative minor of the key of C major.
The key of E minor. This key is the relative minor of the key of G major.
The key of D minor. This key is the relative minor of the key of C major.

The key signature for each of the three popular minor keys is shown in Ex. 16.

Ex. 16 Key signatures for the three popular minor keys

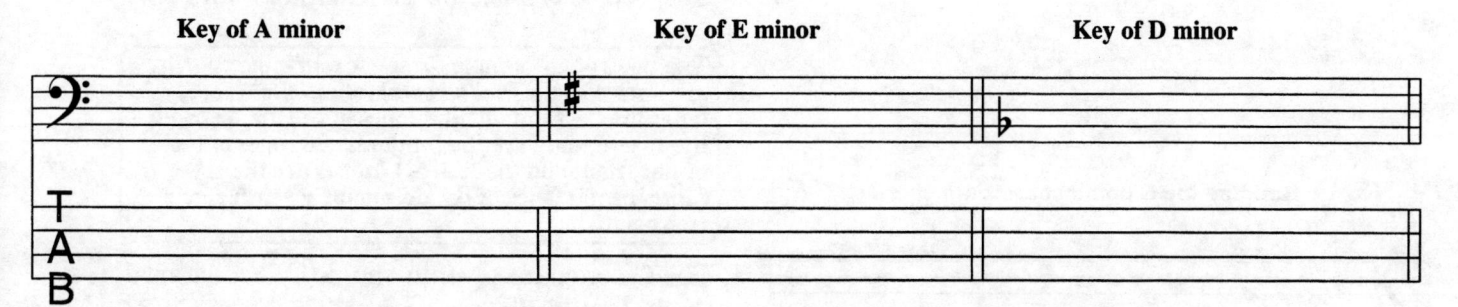

Key of A minor   Key of E minor   Key of D minor

If the same key signature can be shared by a major and a minor key, how do you tell what key a song is in? It's usually pretty easy to do this. In the first place, minor-key songs produce a "lonesome" sound in comparison to major-key songs, which have a "brighter" sound.

Another test: Check the last chord in the song. The final chord almost always reveals the key. For instance, if there are no sharps or flats in the key signature and the last chord is A minor, the song is probably in the key of A minor.

Chords

Harmony is produced by the simultaneous sounding of two or more tones. A *chord* is a group of three or more musical tones sounded together.

Three *types* of chords are used extensively in country music: 1) *major chords*; 2) *minor chords*, and 3) *dominant seventh chords*.

The following examples of the three types of chords will be based on the chords C, C minor, and C7.

1) The major chord (C) contains the <u>first, third, and fifth tones</u> of the corresponding <u>major scale</u> (Ex. 17).
2) The minor chord (Cm or Cmi) contains the <u>first, flatted third, and fifth tones</u> of the corresponding <u>major scale</u> (Ex. 18).
3) The dominant seventh chord (C7) contains the *first, third, fifth, and flatted seventh tones* of the corresponding <u>major scale</u> (Ex. 19).

Ex. 17 Building the C major chord (C)

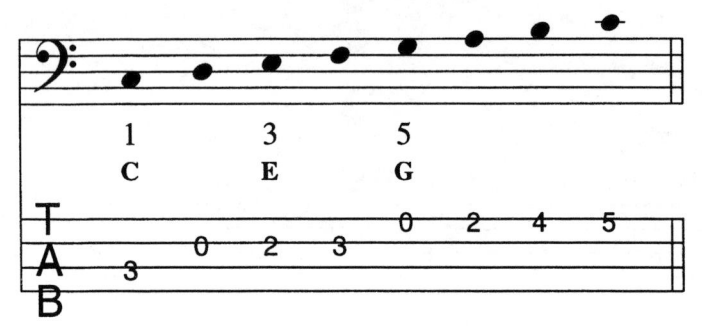

1. The C major chord (C) contains the notes C-E-G.
2. A three-note chord is known as a *triad*.
3. The C chord is a *major triad*.
4. The *formula* for a major triad is 1-3-5.
5. The major triad formula, 1-3-5, can be applied to any major scale. For example, the 1st, 3rd, and 5th tones of the G scale (G-B-D, respectively) make up the G major chord (G).

> The first note (1) of any chord is known as the *root*.
> The root note is the most important note in the chord.

Ex. 18 Building the C minor chord (Cm)

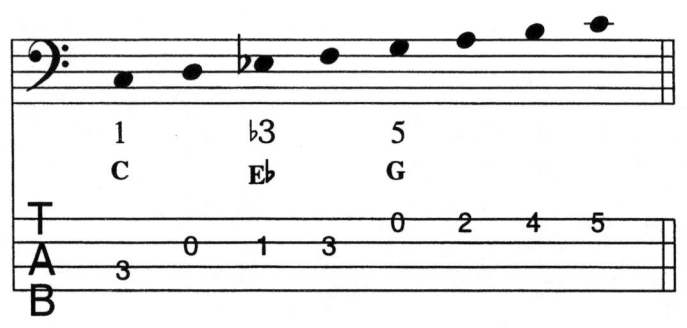

1. The C minor chord (Cm) contains the notes C-E♭-G.
2. The C minor chord is a *minor triad*.
3. The formula for a minor triad is 1-♭3-5.
4. The term *flatted third* (♭3) means that the third tone of the scale is lowered by one-half step.
5. The minor triad formula, 1-♭3-5, can be applied to any major scale. For example, the 1st, flatted 3rd, and 5th tones of the G scale (G-B♭-D, respectively) make up the G minor chord (Gm).

> The notes of any simple three- or four-note chord are known as the *fundamental* tones. The 1, 3, 5, tones are the fundamental tones of the major triad; the 1, ♭3, 5 tones are the fundamental tones of the minor triad; and the 1, 3, 5, ♭7 tones are the fundamental tones of the dominant seventh chord (see below).

Ex. 19 Building the C dominant seventh chord (C7)

1. The C dominant seventh chord (C7) contains the notes C-E-G-B♭.
2. The formula for a dominant seventh chord is 1-3-5-♭7.
3. The term *flatted seventh* (♭7) means the seventh tone of the scale is lowered by one-half step.
4. The dominant seventh chord formula, 1-3-5-♭7, can be applied to any major scale. For example, the 1st, 3rd, 5th, and flatted 7th tones of the G major scale (G-B-D-F) produce the G7 chord.

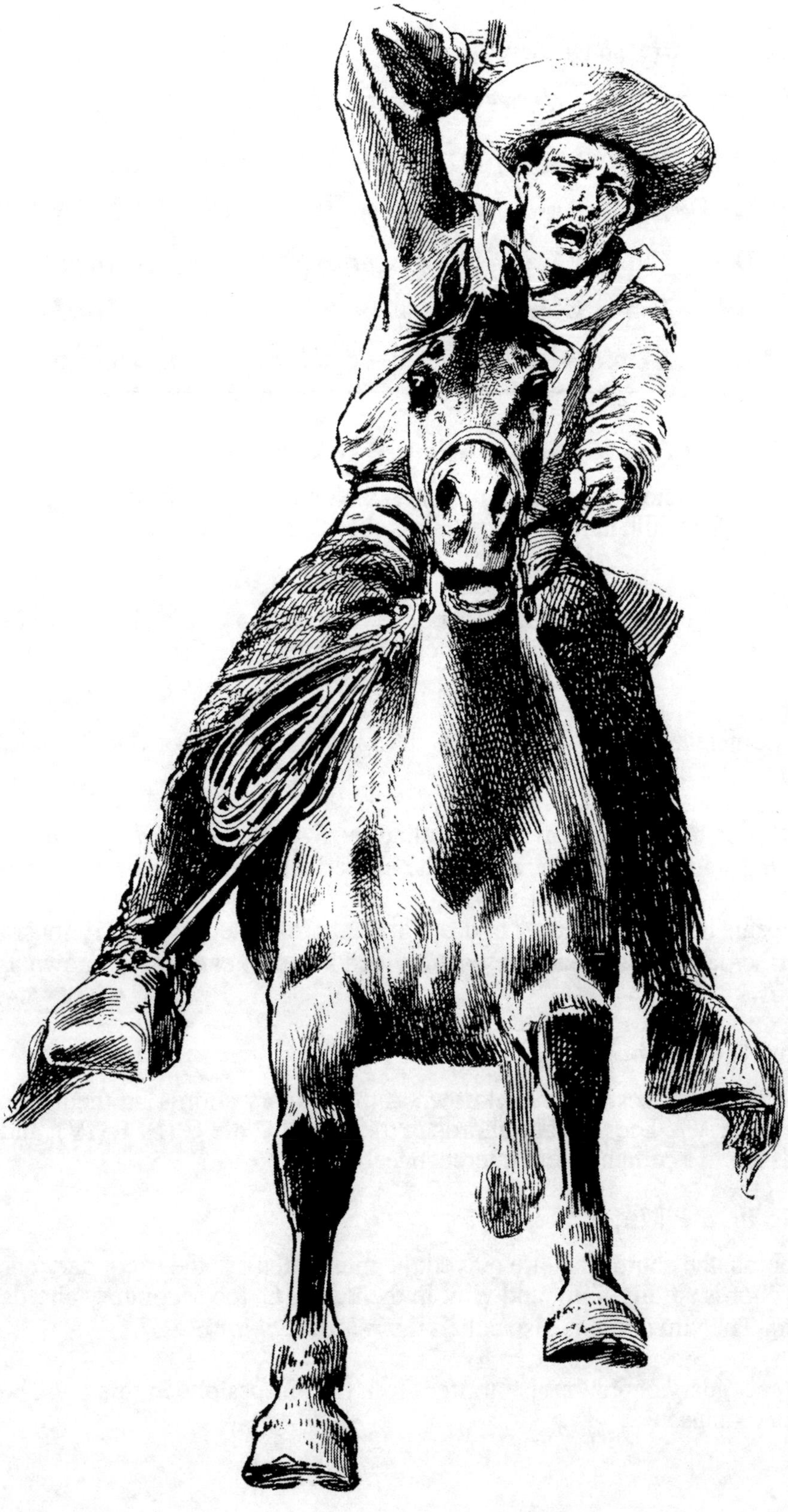

Principal Chords in the Major Keys

Every major and minor key contains seven chords known as the *principal chords* of that key. Each of the seven principal chords is built on (or "rooted in") a tone of the corresponding scale. The principal chords in the five popular major keys are shown in Ex. 20.

Ex. 20   Principal chords in five major keys

	I	iim	iiim	IV	V or V7	vim	viim♭5
Key of C major:	C	Dm	Em	F	G or G7	Am	Bm♭5
Key of G major:	G	Am	Bm	C	D or D7	Em	F♯m♭5
Key of D major:	D	Em	F♯m	G	A or A7	Bm	C♯m♭5
Key of A major:	A	Bm	C♯m	D	E or E7	F♯m	G♯m♭5
Key of E major:	E	F♯m	G♯m	A	B or B7	C♯m	D♯m♭5

Identifying the Chords (The Nashville Number System)

At the top of each column of chords is a Roman numeral. Numerals for major and dominant chords appear in the uppercase (I, IV, V7), while numerals for minor chords appear in the lowercase (im, iiim, vim, viim♭5).

The first part of each numeral is a number that identifies the position of the chord root in the scale. For example, I means that the root of the C chord (which is, of course, the C note) is the first note in the C scale.

Some of the Roman numerals have a suffix such as m (minor), m♭5 (minor flat 5), and 7. However, major triads (C, F, G, etc.) do not carry a suffix.

This system of identifying chord function can be called the *Roman Numeral System*. Country musicians use the term *Nashville Number System* to refer to the numerical identification of chords.

The viim♭5 chord appears here as a "theory" chord, but it is rarely used in country music. The six important (for our purposes) principal chords in each key are divided into two categories known as *primary chords* and *secondary chords*.

Primary Chords in the Major Keys

The chords that are played the most often are known as the primary chords. In the major keys, the primary chords are I, IV, and V or V7. The primary chords in the key of C are C (I), F (IV), and G (V) or G7 (V7). The V and V7 chords are to a certain extent interchangeable.

Secondary Chords in the Major Keys

After the primary chords, the chords that are played the most often are the secondary chords. In the major keys, the secondary chords are iim, iiim, and vim. In the key of C, the secondary chords are: Dm (iim), Em (iiim), and Am (vim). The vim chord is also called the *relative minor chord*.

The viim♭5 is also a secondary chord, but is omitted from the discussions in this book because it is almost never heard in country songs.

Principal Chords in the Natural Minor Keys

The principal chords in the three popular <u>natural minor</u> keys are shown in Ex. 21.

Ex. 21 Principal chords in three minor keys

	im	iim♭5	bIII	ivm	vm or V7	♭VI	♭VII
Key of A minor:	Am	Bm♭5	C	Dm	Em or E7	F	G
Key of E minor:	Em	F#m♭5	G	Am	Bm or B7	C	D
Key of D minor:	Dm	Em♭5	F	Gm	Am or A7	B♭	C

The iim♭5 chord is listed here as a "theory" chord, but it is rarely used in country music. We will divide the six remaining chords into the categories of primary and secondary.

Primary Chords in the Natural Minor Keys

In any natural minor key, the primary chords are im, ivm, and vm <u>or</u> V7. Thus, the primary chords in the key of Am are Am (im), Dm (ivm), and Em (vm) or E7 (V7).

The vm and V7 chords are not interchangeable like the V and V7 chords are. If the music for a song in C major says to play a G7 chord (V7), a G chord (IV) can also be played. If the same music has a G chord, there is a strong chance that a G7 might work just as well (or better). However, vm and V7 are distinct harmonies and are not directly interchangeable in any key.

Secondary Chords in the Natural Minor Keys

The secondary chords in the minor keys are ♭III, ♭VI, and ♭VII. In the key of A minor, these chords are C, F, and G, respectively.

The flat sign is used as a prefix when the flat reflects the position of a single tone, or the root tone of a chord, in the corresponding <u>major</u> scale. For example, the third tone of the A major scale is C#. If we lower C# by a half-step, it becomes C. The C note is the "flatted third (♭3) of A."

For more information about chord theory, chord progressions, and scales, see the following Mel Bay book/CD sets by Larry McCabe:

You Can Teach Yourself Song Writing™. This book/CD set teaches essential music theory in an interesting, easy to understand collection of songs and examples. The 90 tracks of music on the CD make it easy to absorb the concepts presented in the book.

101 Amazing Jazz Bass Patterns. Appendix 1, <u>Basic Theory for the Jazz Musician</u>, contains an excellent 10-page discussion on chord theory, scale tones, and other important concepts that are beyond the scope of the present discussion.

Bass Patterns

The country bass player has two main responsibilities:

1) Outline the fundamental tones of the chord.
2) Keep a steady beat.

Examples 22-41 show a number of typical country bass patterns. Examples include the following:

1) Patterns that normally can be applied to only one type of chord (for example, C7 but not C or Cm).
2) Patterns that can be applied to more than one type of chord.
3) Patterns that are used with specific chord changes (progressions).
4) Patterns in cut time (two-beat), 4/4 time, and 3/4 time.

The intervals for each pattern are shown below the music staff, above the tablature.

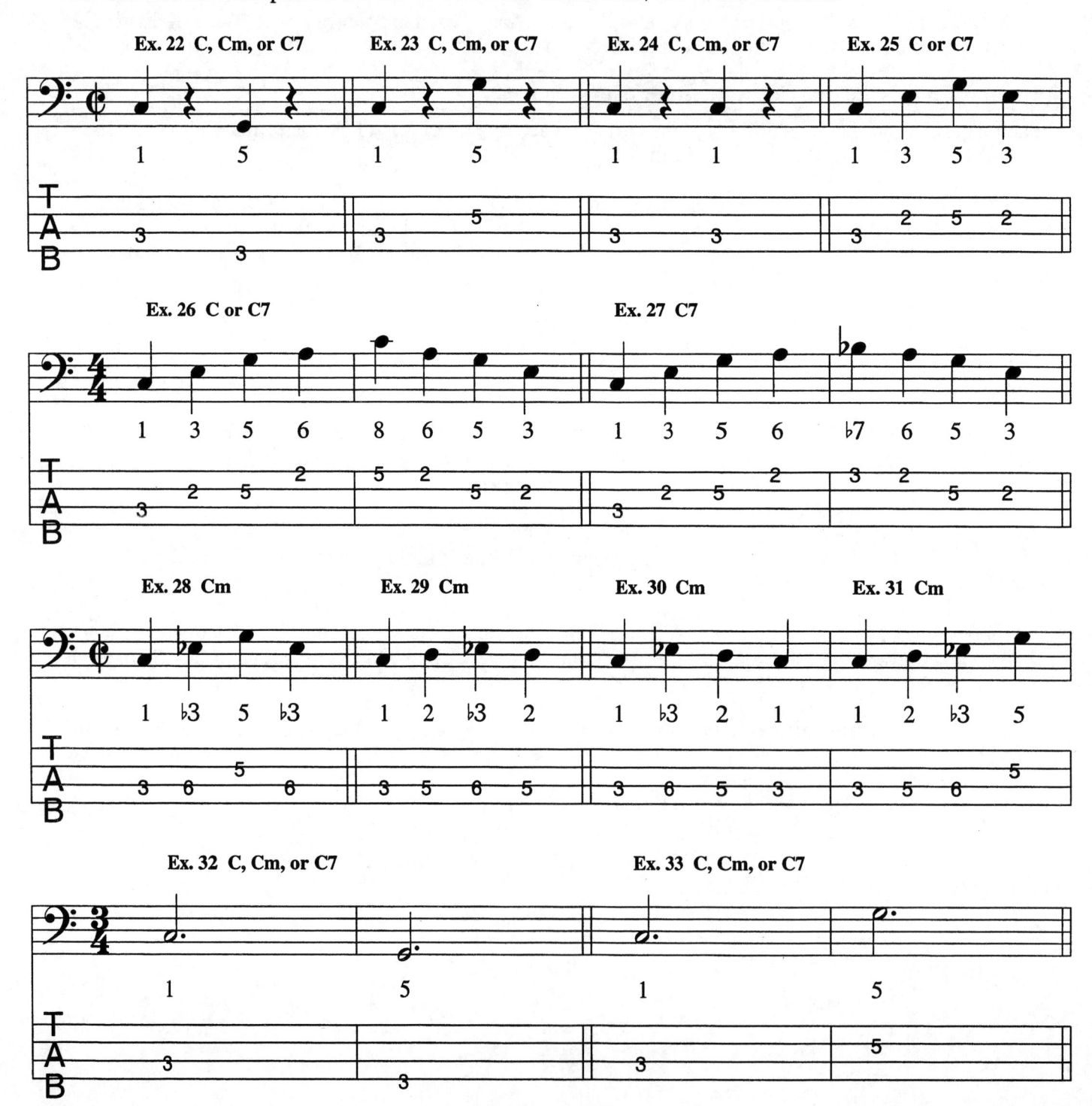

Ex. 34 C, Cm, or C7

Ex. 35 C, Cm, or C7

Ex. 36 The sixth tone works well with both major and dominant chords (and sometimes with minor chords). The sixth of C is A; The sixth of G is E; The sixth of F is D; etc.

Ex. 37 The third is usually used in country bass lines only when it is moving somewhere.

Ex. 38 The tone that is a 1/2 step below the root of the target chord is called a lower neighbor tone. A lower neighbor is often used as an approach to the root tone of the target chord (the target chord is the "next" chord).

Ex. 39 The third of G7 is also the lower neighbor of the root tone of the C chord.

Ex. 40 The 5th tone of the target chord is often played as an approach tone.

Ex. 41 The root of G7 is also the 5th of C.

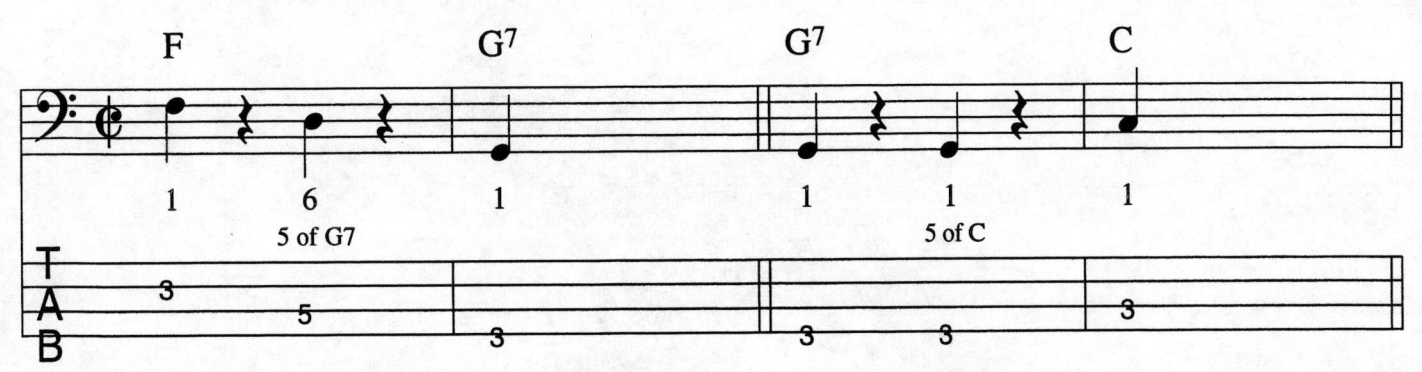

INDEX

All the Good Times Are Past and Gone 10
Amazing Grace 9
Angel Band 12
Careless Love 46
Corrine, Corrina 47
Cotton–Eyed Joe 30
Cripple Creek 27
Don't Let Your Deal Go Down 22
Hangman, Hangman 42
Home on the Range 18
Knoxville Girl 14
New River Train 32
Roll in My Sweet Baby's Arms 28
Salty Dog 26
Sinner Man 38
St. James Infirmary 48
Sweet Hour of Prayer 16
Wabash Cannonball 34
Wayfarin' Stranger 40
Will the Circle Be Unbroken 24
Worried Man Blues 44
Wreck of the Old '97 21